The Super You

Unlocking And Living With Your Highest
Level Of Confidence

Dre "DreAllDay" Baldwin

ISBN: 9781501092589

Dre Baldwin

CONTENTS

More By Dre Baldwin 47

The Super You

Disclaimer

First a disclaimer, so you know exactly what you're getting into with this book.

When I was a child, there were these color-by-numbers coloring books we would play with. Each page would have a picture of, say, a bear. And the bear would have different areas of its body marked by a number. There was a little box in the corner of the page that told you which colors referred to each number. So if the number "1" was green, you colored all the corresponding 1s on the page in green. Then you did the same with black, red, yellow and the rest. After coloring in all the numbered sections, you'd have a perfectly colored picture to admire. There was no thinking or real-life application necessary. Just do what the damn book said, step by step, and everything would be perfect.

The Super You is not a coloring book.

My goals in writing this book are to:

1.   Give you insight into the phenomenon of confidence by explaining what it is, where it comes from, when you can use it to your advantage, and how it is developed, strengthened and weakened.

2.   Prepare you to apply what you read in real life, learning instinctively when to use each tool in your box, since no two situations are ever exactly the same.

3.   Leave you with The Super You, the version of you who has the confidence to think and say and do all of the things you've considered but haven't dared trying.

That's what this book is.

What I am not doing: Holding you by the hand and giving you a series of if-then loops (*"if this happens, do this..." "If she does this, you say this..."*) on how to conduct yourself.

Each one of us is a unique individual, with a unique mental wiring and a unique personality. Everything you read in this book, you will apply to your life as it fits *you*. Confidence is an internal energy that radiates outward. This is true for both the introverted and the extroverted amongst us. We all have both sides within us, that we display at different times depending on the situation. Confidence is not about being the-life-of-the-party personality every day; if that is not you, don't try to make it you. That would be a waste of time and energy. No one would believe you anyway, when you're being someone you're not — people can read it off of you. This is a very important point when it comes to confidence; we will discuss it in detail later in this book.

A core principle of confidence is staying 100% true to yourself. The Super You is the new, supremely confident version of you, but it is still YOU. Always remember this. You don't need me, nor anyone else, telling you exactly what to do, how, or when to do it. Your confidence will be rooted in knowing that you can look to, feed off of, and depend on yourself. Not another person, not some inanimate object, and not a book (though I will recommend you coming back to this book in the future to keep your skills sharp).

You will be secure and strong based on your belief of yourself, not what anyone else thinks. Your Super You confidence will not be based on your belief in other people. On the contrary, The Super You will invoke feelings of *belief from others in you.* You won't be running to someone else every time some challenge stands in front of you. You will be the person other people look to when *they* need reassurance. As Tim Grover says in *Relentless,* when everyone is hitting the "In case of emergency" button, they're all looking for you. That's my goal in writing or recording or speaking anything related to motivation: To empower you to be better as yourself, to the point that you look inward, not outward.

Having unshakeable confidence in yourself is a damn good place to begin, wouldn't you agree?

The Super You is not an entertainment read that you enjoy and toss to the side; this is an inform-and-strategize manifesto. Take the information you read here, think deeply about it, and strategize to use it in your real, everyday interactions with real, live people. You will not become confident by simply reading a fucking book. Confidence comes from actions, not thoughts.

Let me repeat that:

You will not become confident by simply reading a fucking book. Confidence comes from actions, not thoughts.

Confidence is, simply defined, a belief in your ability to do things. Thus, confidence comes from action. You take action, analyze your outcomes, evaluate, and base your future actions on what you've learned. If you think about it, this is how we do every single thing in our lives.

You cannot read or think or YouTube-watch your way to confidence. What you will learn in The Super You is not passive learning. I will give you actionable and applicable information that you will take into your personal interactions. This book will have you taking actions aimed at improving your belief in yourself. Confidence -- belief in your abilities -- is rooted not in the thinking, but in the doing.

This book is about the doing.

Now that that's out of the way, let's get into it.

Introduction

Confidence is the basis of every single thing you do. Walking, eating, driving a car, reading a book -- you do these things without thinking about them, because you're innately sure of your ability to do so. Confidence is what allows you to unconsciously do hundreds of things every single day, and you don't need to stop and ask yourself *if* you're able to do them.

You also have confidence in things and people outside of yourself. You buy items online with the confidence that the seller isn't going to scam you and run off with your money. You are confident about the restaurant food you ate last night. Even though you don't know who prepared the food and you didn't witness the process, you happily cleaned the plate when the waiter brought your meal out. You were confident in the driving skills of the person whose car you got into last week. You are confident that the paycheck you just took to the bank will clear and deposit into your account.

You have more confidence, in many more areas, than you think you do. This book's goal is for you to have that same confidence, consciously and unconsciously, in yourself.

***

Confidence is more than important. It's every-damn-thing. Being exceptionally talented or skilled is worthless without the confidence to actually show those skills when it's time to.

This book is not just about your basic understanding and application of confidence. This book is about the level of confidence that separates you from everyone around you. This book is about the level of confidence that pushes you to out-shine your peers (and leave them behind for new peers, if necessary). It's about a level of confidence that forces other people to, literally and figuratively, step aside and let you through. I'm talking about the level of confidence that takes you from looking at other people and wishing to be like them, to making other people wish to be like YOU. The level of confidence I'm talking about is what we'll call the Super You.

What exactly is the Super You? The Super You is the You that you're afraid of being.

The Super You Is The You That You're Afraid Of Being.

You will understand exactly why the above statement is true as you read this book. The only thing between Current

You and Super You is what you innately believe about yourself. Nothing more, nothing less.

Think of all the wild, ambitious ideas you have ever had for your life — things you dream of doing, being, having. Just by the practice of thinking about them, those ideas are real: Something you saw or heard or experienced birthed that vision. Which, in turn, means it's possible. Now, think of how different your everyday life would be if you started taking the necessary actions to make all of those ideas happen. That's the Super You. The only thing between Current You and You that will take those actions, is an increased level of confidence. You will develop that confidence through reading and applying what you read in this book.

The Super You Is The Version Of You That You're Afraid Of Being.

Or, rather, the You that a *fear of success* is holding you back from.

The high level of success that comes with becoming The Super You brings some darkness. You've heard the cliché that it's lonely at the top, right? Well, loneliness is dark. The more successful you push yourself to be, the fewer people who will relate to you. Most will not understand the way you think, the actions you're taking, and the sacrifices you're making.

Another reason for the darkness: once you have shown you can reach that high level, that's what everyone will be expecting of you. When you show people what you are capable of, in their eyes you create a new standard for yourself. And living up to that standard can be uncomfortable.

Knowing that you'll have to be that star — that person on top and out in front — every day, is a burden that most would rather not carry. Most people would choose to be comfortable, or "good enough". Knowing those expectations, that everyone is depending on you to lead and deliver, to be as good as you've shown you can be, is a choice. It's a choice to step into that lonely darkness.

As kids, we run to mommy and daddy when we're afraid of the dark. As adults, many of us never lose that fear. Instead of parents, we run to the comfort and safety of remaining average and "good enough".

The Super You Is The Version Of You That You're Afraid Of Being.

It's the You that you stop short of expressing at those times when it seems as if everything in your life, business and personal, is flowing in the right direction. Attention and the spotlight are finding you. You're putting on a show, so to speak, with your life and your way of thinking, acting and being. You're a leader, whether you chose to be or not.

Think of those times when you have such a good flow of successes, that people start paying extra attention to you. You know exactly what I'm talking about: Everyone's watching to see what you'll do next. They watch because success draws attention: Everyone wants it, at least in theory. Performing (thinking, acting, being) at this level when in this flow, is scary to most people. This is why we stop *ourselves* short and remain in our comfort zones. Someone actually *doing it,* confidently and intentionally going after success, draws attention. The majority of people in your life will happily sit on the sidelines and watch you live that life, rather than step into the darkness themselves. Many people would rather be average and comfortable. Comfort leads to complacency. The Super You is not complacent.

Just so we're clear: Becoming the Super You *does* incur a risk. The risk that people will question just who the hell you think you are. The risk that people will actively attempt to thwart you from becoming a person that makes *them* feel small about themselves. The risk that at some moment when the light is shining on you, you'll panic and retreat to the comfort of the Old (Current) You. The risk of carrying the expectations. Walking in the darkness. You will be walking in darkness. If the path was well lit, clear and safe, there would be no need for this book, because *everyone* would walk that path. No matter how many people know about the path, only a select few even want to take this walk.

By picking up this book, you've already identified yourself as one of them.

People will stop and watch when they see you doing what they're afraid to do. And many times they will, secretly or openly, hope that you fail.

Why? Because you failing will make them feel better about themselves. You tapping into that Super You will make a lot of people, even for a brief moment, look inward and wonder what *they're* missing. And remember: most people prefer comfort. So what do they do, in this moment of self-reflection and discomfort? They go to where it's safe. They look outward and try really hard to find fault with you, wanting to see you fail, so they can relieve the pain of having to look inward and question what's wrong with themselves.

Why do you think people take such joy at the downfalls of famous people?

Why do celebrities command our attention? First, you should understand what that kind of attention is: A white-hot heat shining on you, everywhere you go, everything you do and every word you say. Heat is hot, and many people, upon feeling that heat for something they did or said — even if they meant to do it — melt under that heat and go scurrying back into the shade of anonymity, where it's cool and comfortable.

Celebrities are, for the most part, not much more talented than your average Joe or Jane. They feel that heat of attention the same way anyone else would. What makes that celebrity a celebrity, is that they are not afraid of the heat of all that attention that comes from them doing exactly what they want to do with their lives and *being 100% unapologetic about it.* They know you're watching. They know that many people are secretly praying on their downfall. And they live the life they want to live anyway.

I'm not telling you that you need to try and become a celebrity. Celebrities are just an example of what happens when you take your confidence to the fullest extent. There are plenty of people out there whom you will never hear of, who are living as the Super-You version of themselves. This book is not about the pursuit of fame.

What I am saying is this: There are self-limiting factors within your conscious and subconscious mind that are keeping you from being the best You. This book is about identifying and destroying those self-imposed limits (and yes, they are ALL created and maintained by your own thinking).

Does this sound dangerous to you? Risky and unsafe? I understand your concern, but it's really not dangerous at all, and I'll tell you why. You are much more likely, in life, to stop short of how good you could be than you are likely of going too far.

You are much more likely to stop short of how good you could be than you are likely of going too far.

This book is about seeing what happens when we decide to go too far, take that extra step beyond "good enough" and see just how good we can really be.

Again, this isn't for everyone. Some people prefer the safety and comfort of living life on their front porch, so to speak.

They can keep the lights on and be relatively comfortable. No darkness to worry about. And that's where they belong.

This book was not written for them. It was written for you.

The Super You is not about being flawless, never messing up or never experiencing failure again — that is nearly impossible. On the contrary, people who live the life of the Super You aren't afraid of stepping into something that might fail; only average people are afraid of failing. The failures you deal with provide the lessons and real-world experience required for repeated big successes in life. Failure is a necessary prerequisite for the future accomplishments that make people stop and pay attention to you.

Why? Because most people will stay on the sidelines, afraid of what people will say or think if they fail. Thus, they never try anything and never accomplish anything meaningful, save for "not failing". We have a term for people who consider not failing to be an accomplishment: Losers. You probably know many of these people. You may have even been one of them at some point. That time has passed. Now, it's time for The Super You.

The Super You is about not being afraid of failure, embracing the learning experience, and taking it in stride just as easily as you take your successes. The way you handle failure is one crucial element of the Super You. Remember that most people scale back their ambitions or quit, when visited by failure or its possibility.

No one likes to fail, but we have all done it at times and we will all fail again as long as we keep living and pushing our limits. Despite the fact that we have all experienced failure, some people develop an unhealthy fear of failure that prevents them from trying anything further in their lives. They would rather stay in safety and try nothing, than to try and go for anything that *might not* succeed. These are the same people who will ridicule and belittle you for failing, while they stay comfortably on the sidelines in life, watching everyone pass them by while they hold on to the little that they have.

These people are Losers. You will find these people slowly drifting away from your life as you transform into The Super You.

The Super You is for you to fully embrace the fact that you could, possibly, wildly succeed at something. It's not that you don't *know* you could succeed, it's that you don't know if you even *want to* succeed... too much. Because with success comes the attention we talked about. With success comes competition. With success comes people watching you, expecting you to do it again. With success comes responsibility, because people will want to mimic you in some way and will be following everything you do. With success comes the mental burden you put on yourself, knowing that people are expecting you to repeat your achievements. With success comes the darkness.

How many people do you know whose accomplishments far exceed their natural abilities? (These people, most of the time without even knowing it, have tapped into their Super Selves.)

Who do you know who always seems so very sure of themselves, even when the situation doesn't look great? That's the Super You at work.

How many people have you seen do or say something and thought to yourself, 'I wish I had the balls/confidence/moxie to do what she just did'? It doesn't have to be a wish. That's your Super You whispering in your ear, letting you know that it's available to you. This book will have you making conscious use of that whisper.

Conversely, how many people do you know (or know of) who seem to underachieve in everything they do? You know, those people who are not exactly failures, but seem to always leave something on the table?

How many times have you seen a highly skilled or supremely talented person lose to a lesser individual in a high-pressure moment on a big stage?

Who do you know (of) who always leaves you feeling that they're holding something back? You look at what they do or have done and wonder, why they didn't do more with the tools they have at their disposal? What are they missing?

Confidence is the key element behind all of these situations, positive and negative. An increase in confidence will lead to you attempting to do more, and in turn accomplishing more. The stronger you feel about your ability to do things, the more you'll do and the better you'll do them. This applies to any of life's endeavors. Your confidence level essentially determines your life. The Super You is confidence on undetectable, designer steroids.

This book will start by deconstructing confidence — what it is, and how it feels to have it. Then, we'll get into constructing your confidence. Next, I'll share things you can consciously apply to your everyday life to build your confidence, even if you're starting at zero (ever heard of "Fake it 'til you make it"? There's nothing fake about that at all. I'll show you why and how).

Then we get into the Super You: where it comes from, what it means and how you'll develop and use yours. Finally, I will end with applicable practices for building and maintaining your confidence, and an appendix of exercises to use should your confidence ever slip.

Step into the darkness.

What Confidence Looks And Feels Like

Think of a time when all eyes were on you, and you loved every second of it. You weren't nervous about the attention. In fact, whatever it is you did to draw attention, you wanted to do even more of it. Your mentality was, *they're all watching, and they should be.*

You know this feeling because you have been there before. Heading into a situation, you believed in your ability, and you executed. Then, after the fact, everyone believed. Just how you knew it would go.

That's confidence.

You walked boldly into every situation. No nervousness, no insecurity. Nothing anyone said or did could bother you. Everything in your path, no matter its intentions in being there, just drove you more and harder, like a brush fire sweeping through the forest. Anything in the way just made the blaze stronger.

When your confidence is high, there's no fear in addressing tough issues or taking on challenging tasks. There's no timidity. When you want something, you verbalize what you want and find ways to get it. In communicating, you look people in the eye and speak loud and clear when you have something to say. There is no intimidation — you see people exactly as they are and not for what they present themselves to be. People have the utmost respect for you and the way you carry yourself -- though they never say it, you can feel it.

You're not afraid of failing. Failure is a part of life that happens to everyone. You embrace your failures as life lessons, because they represent the fact that you've tried something that those people on the sidelines would never have the gall to attempt. All of the most successful people you know of and follow have had many more failures than successes, but the successes would never have happened without the failures to teach them, toughen them up, and prepare them for the next challenge.

***

When you walk into a room, your body language and the look in your eye at that exact moment gives everyone a snap judgement of you. Remember that the body follows the mind: whatever you are thinking and feeling about yourself, your physical presentation will express it perfectly. The eyes -- the windows to the human soul -- never lie. Human beings make unconscious judgements every day, in every situation. Whether they should pet or run from the dog, if their significant other is in a good mood or of something is amiss. We make these decisions without thought and in a split second. You may know them by another word: instincts. People make instinctive judgements about your level of confidence as soon as they encounter you, even from afar and without conversation. Knowing this, understand and remember: Your confidence is communicated by the way you carry yourself.

Your confidence is communicated by the way you carry yourself.

Have you ever seen a person walk into a room and orally announce their current level of confidence out loud? Probably not. And even if someone did, we wouldn't believe them. Their body language and demeanor has already told us everything we needed to know. No one ever has to make an announcement about how they feel. As soon as we encounter a person, we make a decision about that person and how they view themselves. And since we unconsciously do this with every person we see, it would be smart to make sure the impression you communicate is the one you want people to have of you. Makes sense, right?

Confidence is an *unshakable belief in what you can do*. You've decided who you are and what's going to happen. Externalities, like what someone else does or says, changes in the weather, and traffic on the road, don't change your decision. Confidence is a decision that you believe in yourself and what you can do. When something gets in your way, you work over it or around it or through it. External factors don't affect your decision; your decision affects external factors. You tell your feelings how to feel. *This is what it is, and this is how it's going to be.*

Confidence is stable and calm. Confidence doesn't need reassurance or approval from anyone else. Confidence commands the room and sets the tone. Confidence doesn't wait for outcomes, confidence determines outcomes.

How Weak Confidence Crippled Me, And How I Destroyed It

Around the age of five, my mother noticed that something may have been wrong with my vision because of the way I blinked when I watched TV. The eye doctor prescribed me glasses, thick bifocals to be exact. The stage was set for a lack of confidence within me that would last for years.

At this time, the late 80s to early 90s, there was a popular TV show called *Family Matters*. The main character was a young kid named Steve Urkel. Steve was annoying and awkward, with thick eyeglasses and tight-fitting clothes (back when it wasn't cool to have tight-fitting clothes). Steve was infatuated with Laura, the pretty girl next door who was also Steve's classmate. But Laura, who was the most popular girl in school, had no affinity or use for the lovable but annoying nerd-next-door.

One episode per season on Family Matters, Steve would disappear and his "cousin" and alter ego, Stephon Urkell ("er-kell") would show up next door, always finding time to stop by and say hello to Laura. Stephon was cool, smooth, and supremely confident. He *commanded the room*. Stephon always said the right thing at the right time, and nothing seemed to ever bother him. His attitude seemed to control situations more than the situations controlled his attitude.

Laura was spellbound by Stephon. Shit, *I* was spellbound by Stephon. He was everything I wished I could be.

Well, wishing and being are two completely different things.

In the fourth grade, I wore tight-fitting clothes, thanks to our mandated school uniforms, that were always just a *bit* too small. My glasses had thick lenses and a geeky-looking Croakies strap that wrapped around the back of my head, keeping them securely on my face so they didn't fall off and break. I knew I liked girls, but back then, I was more of an amusement to females rather than a serious "like" interest, like some of my friends were.

Older boys at school bullied and made fun of me. At a candy store named Amy Six that was one block away from my school, I would always spend a dollar or two every afternoon. One day I was walking home with a small sandwich baggie full of sweets, eating them one piece at a time, when two older boys started following me. One of them asked me to share my candy with him, but I refused. They caught up to me at the front steps of my house and the boy snatched the entire bag out of my hand and jogged off, leaving me standing there crying. That same boy walked right up to me the next day and asked me about the situation, knowing that he was not in any danger of retaliation (fortunately this bully had a conscience; he didn't take anything from me again).

The candy, I could buy more of. But the humiliation and embarrassment of having someone take something from me, and all three parties involved — me, my mother (whom I came home crying to), and the bully — knowing that I wasn't going to do a damn thing about it was what hurt the most.

During that same school year, there was a group of older girls, sixth or seventh graders, who would sit on the steps of a house that was on my route home. These girls would laugh hysterically at the sight of me walking by, every single day after school, just due to my appearance.

That type of humiliation of being picked on and laughed at and called a geek or nerd (again, back when it was not cool to be either) eroded my confidence like the waves of the ocean grinding rocks into sand. Aside from doing schoolwork, driveway kickball games and playing Nintendo, I wasn't confident about anything at all.

During fifth grade, then attending a new school, I made the switch from glasses to contact lenses. I looked different now and was no longer a punchline for older kids. I even started to generate some interest from females. What I found out, though, was that the difference between Steve and Stephon from *Family Matters* wasn't the clothes and the cologne and the removal of the glasses. It was the way Stephon carried himself, which told everyone else how to feel about him.

Confidence. Stephon's nice clothes and pretty face meant nothing without all that damn *confidence*.

Despite my new no-glasses look and (very) mild female attention, I was still the same self-conscious geek who figured he would never become like Stephon.

I didn't get any of the girls I ever fantasized about or wanted. I didn't see myself as having much reach socially. I wasn't one of the cool kids. Had I even attempted to aim a bit higher for myself, the reputation I had established, or had established for me to that point by my peers, had solidified. First impressions last. My peers' crystallized perception of me, combined with my own, wouldn't have allowed me to go beyond my normal place.

The way you walk into a room is the way you'll be in that room, and it's the way you'll walk out of that room.

By high school, I had started to play basketball regularly and began to attain some recognition for my play, at least at my neighborhood park. Basketball was, to that point, the thing I was best at. Despite this revelation, I had not yet done anything notable as a basketball player.

So, the thing that I felt was my meal ticket to confidence, was also a dose of confidence-shattering reality.

Despite some neighborhood basketball notoriety, success was harder to come by on the court at school, where the opportunities were fewer and further between. I tried and failed, three times, at varsity basketball tryouts (we had no junior varsity program, so it was varsity-or-bust). I finally made the team as a senior and sat the bench all season. When I graduated, I knew that basketball was my best shot at recognition in this world. But there was no one around me who saw a future in hoops for me.

For a year though, without even knowing it, I'd been using a technique that I didn't even know was one of the most important factors in creating your future: Visualization. As a high school senior, I saw something in my future that was completely different from my present. The vision was clear enough that I could feel it. Feeling it so consistently led to me actually believing it. And when you believe in a vision, you leave yourself and the universe no choice but for you to live it out.

Next, I'll explain how I found and began to use visualization, what exactly I did, why it worked for me, and how it will work for you.

How I Began To Construct The Confident Me, And Change My Life

I read a book in my teens — I think it was *The 7 Habits of Highly Effective People* by Stephen Covey — in which the author suggested an experiment.

You're standing outside on the sidewalk of wherever you happen to be, right at this moment. Looking down the street, you see someone walking towards you. This person appears to be somewhat familiar, but you cannot make out who exactly they are. As they get closer, you can see who it is: It's you! Not just you, but you five years from now.

Take a look at your future self. Who are you as a person? What have you achieved? Who do you know? Who knows you? What do people say about you when you're not around? How do you feel about yourself? What has changed about you? What are you proud of? What do you look like? How do you walk? How do you talk? How confident are you and why?

I did this exercise as I read the book. I had no idea back then that I already possessed a strong, intuitive feel for the practice of visualization. This was a simple visualization exercise. Back then, I didn't even know that visualization was what I was doing. But I believed in the exercise and I imagined my future self, answering all of those questions. I had even imagined exactly where I was standing, right at the bottom of the steps of the house I grew up in.

The future me was coming up Dorset Street. A bit taller and clearly, even form half a block away, more muscular and defined through the arms and chest. Future Me had a bop in his step. His (my) confidence was palpable even before I could clearly make out the face. Future Me was successful as a basketball player, confident with the females, sure of himself as a man in dealing with other people on a day-to-day basis. People who had never met Future Me in person knew who he was. Future Me did things and shared ideas that inspired and motivated others. Future Me did what he wanted to do, when he wanted to do it. Complete strangers looked at Future Me and thought, I don't know who this guy is, but he's... *somebody*.

Do the visualization and take note of your Future Self — namely, the changes from who you are now to your five-years-from-now self. What do you want to do, be, have? What do you want people to say about you? What do you want to be able to say about yourself? Who will you become and how will you get there?

See your Future Self. This person is completely of your creation; every detail of that person came from your mind.

Which means, you already know exactly who you want to be. This is the most important exercise I ever did in building my confidence for the future.

When I did this experiment while reading, I made myself *believe* in what I was envisioning. I saw myself growing bigger, walking taller, making a name for myself, having an aura of success and being the type of person whom others looked to as a leader, as an example. I saw Future Me taking all the bold actions necessary to make all of that vision real. I visualized deeply enough that I *felt it*.

All of this is the practice of visualization. As large and complex as our human brains have evolved to be, we still cannot decipher the difference between reality and imagination. Which is why, when we think about the mere possibility of some annoying situation happening to us, we start to feel a bit annoyed. The same applies for happy feelings, anger, and sadness, even the physical feelings of being hot and cold.

This practice is about making your visualizations stronger. You have to train your brain to truly feel and believe your visions, suspending the conscious thoughts that question everything and put our once-vivid imaginations to sleep. When the brain truly believes in the visions we feed it, your brain does what all good servants do: It delivers thoughts, feelings, words and actions that move us towards making those visions a reality.

If I asked you how it would feel to have a billion dollars to your name, you might talk abstractly about what you would do with the money and how you would feel. But if I made you write out a complete, seven-day down-to-the-minute plan for what you would do during your first week with a billion dollars to spend, you would start to feel, sometime during that exercise, like you actually *had* it. Why? Because your brain doesn't know the difference, and all of that pretend-planning, at some point, would start to feel real.

There are only so many times you can remind yourself that you're faking before you start to live out whatever is in your mind. This is what makes great actresses and actors so convincing: When an actor dives deep into the character he portrays on film or TV, it's not acting anymore. He really *becomes* that character. The more detail you allow yourself to go into, the deeper levels of it you allow yourself to think about, the stronger that visualization becomes. Visualize anything enough — make it a habit — and you start to think as if that vision was real. Think it enough, and you start to act on it. Act on it enough, and you *are* it.

I started visualizing whom I would become. How I would grow bigger by lifting weights. How I would keep practicing and become a respected basketball player. How my name would be known by people who had never even met me. I didn't know exactly how I would make that happen, but I felt it, and knew that it would happen. And that visualization made all the difference. From there, all of my thoughts and actions were driven not by my current situation, but by my vision of *where I wanted to be*. By focusing all of my energies on where I wanted to be, I gave myself no choice but to move my life in that direction. Remember: Thoughts, words, and actions are all that make up our days. Whenever you align your thoughts, words and actions to point towards anything — ANYTHING — you will manifest that thing. And when you think about it, there are many circumstances in your life in which you've already successfully done this, positive or negative.

Applying The Practice To Real Life

We are each presented with millions of stimuli every day, all competing for attention or asking you to make a decision. Traffic lights and stop signs. Hot or cold water to wash our hands. Passing glances from strangers in the mall. Which parking spot to take. Over the course of one day, all of these choices add up and deplete our energy levels.

Our bodies have a limit to how much physical output they can produce every day — there is only so much exercising one can do, even for the most well-conditioned athlete. Just the same, our brains have a capacity for work and decisions, and our brains fatigue just the same as our legs or arms get tired. The human brain has a maximum workload of how many thoughts, answers and decisions it can deliver in a day. That's why we sleep at night, take naps when we can, or meditate: Your brain needs a recharge of its batteries.

That being said, the human brain is the most efficient tool known to man. Our brains are always looking for ways to move to optimal efficiency, which means automating as many decisions as possible. We stop at red lights, use hot water to wash our hands and lock the doors when we leave home without ever thinking twice about it, or questioning the act. You have probably done all of these things recently without even thinking about how or why you're doing them. That's the result of your brain automating decisions. It conserves your mental energy for the stuff you'll need to think hard about, and the times when critical thought and decisions are required.

With so many decisions automated, that leftover mental energy will be there, then, for when you need it. To decide where you're going to live when your apartment lease is up. Or how exactly you'll break some shocking news to a loved one. The brain's need to put as many decisions as possible on auto pilot is what leads to stereotypes, which are simply rules we set in our heads based on finite amounts of information. If you're of *this* sex and you wear *these* clothes and I see you in *this* location, you're *this*. If you do *this* combined with *this*, you must be *this*. Because of the mental automation we all do to conserve brain energy, we all have our sets of preconceived notions. Many of our auto-decisions are completely harmless. When someone holds the door for us, they must be a nice person. So we smile and say thanks. If it's too hot inside, you open a window, or turn on the air conditioning. Someone offers a hand to shake, you offer yours.

What does all of this have to do with confidence?

People do not have the mental capacity to sit and question every single thing presented to them every day. It's much easier, and mentally efficient for us, to accept appearances on the surface and believe what people show us. We look, we decide on what we see, and that opinion is set. Undoing the instinctive impression we get from appearances takes a lot of mental energy. This is why first impressions are so important. That first decision we make about another person usually sticks with us forever, no matter what new information is presented.

As far as confidence goes, this is everything.

People judge you, quickly, by the way you present yourself.

People decide about you based on what they see. So keep this in mind: What they see is whatever you decide to show them. We don't have the mental stamina to go around questioning if every person we see is faking it. If you show someone that you're shy or arrogant or gregarious or bold, that's what you become in their eyes. If you show them that you're the most self-assured person in the room, they will believe it. What other information do they have to go off of? Even if or when people get more information about you later on, they will always compare it to their first instinctive decision: the auto-impression that you supplied to them the first time they encountered you.

I understand, though, that this can be a challenge. If you've never *done* anything to be confident *about*, it can be hard to present yourself as confident. This may be one of the reasons you're reading this book.

So what *do* you do if you have no achievements to be self-assured about? If you've never been comfortable talking in front of an audience, how can you appear as if you are? How can you look like you believe you're a "ten" when you have always thought of yourself, and many others see you, as just a "five"?

You fake it. You fake it to the point that you forget that you're tricking yourself.

Next, we will take that visualization of your Future Self, and get so fake it's ridiculous.

Faking It: Why And How It Works

Confidence is all based on belief. Belief in what you can do, belief that you can and will find a way to make things happen. For the most confident amongst us, this comes from having actually done things to be confident about. But for the rest of us, it's hard to believe in yourself when there is nothing around you or in your past that reflects those abilities.

So what does that person, who has no resume of success, do to reflect a trait that is largely based on past accomplishments?

You fake it. You fake it so hard that you arrive at the point where you forget you're faking and it becomes real.

The faking it concept is all about the space you place yourself in mentally. You assume the thought process of a person who has already done the things that are in front of you. Now you know you can do them, because in your mind you have *already* done them. Allow yourself to believe this enough, and you will start to think and act on these thoughts.

When you truly believe in what you're faking, it's as real as you want or allow it to be. Look at the story of Christopher

Columbus, the man who "discovered" America. Columbus was just a merchant back in Spain, not a sailor. Columbus had never led a group of men in his life, in any task. He lacked navigational skills. Upon landing in the New World, Columbus named the people he encountered "Indians," believing he was in India. India would have been in the opposite direction from Spain, where his journey began.

So how did Columbus do it? How did he manage to get financed by the Queen of Spain with 3 ships and all his crew, when he had no credibility whatsoever?

Columbus convinced himself of his own confidence. He faked it to the point that he wasn't faking at all.

When approaching Queen Isabella and her ministers, Columbus asked for three ships and made the demand to be called "Grand Admiral of The Oceanic Sea". He demanded to be named ruler, in the name of Spain, of all lands he discovered. He also demanded to receive 10% of future commerce in all lands he found. Remarkably, Isabella agreed to all of his demands (except the 10%, which she denied in the fine print of their contract. Columbus never read the fine print). Why did she agree to finance this voyage of a mere merchant who had zero experience?

Christopher Columbus presented his requests for the New World voyage as if his demands were a foregone conclusion. He carried himself as if he were destined for greatness. Columbus approached the Queen as if the two were equals, it just so happened that one of them had more money. With nothing else to go off of, Isabella had to believe what was presented to her: this was a man of supreme confidence who knew exactly where he was going and what he wanted. Isabella and everyone else present when Columbus visited the Queen's court had no choice but to believe in Columbus, because Christopher Columbus gave them no other choice.

I read a story by author Tucker Max about his days playing high school basketball. One day in practice, their exasperated coach grew tired of pointing out all of his players' mistakes over and over. So he came up with an idea, a one-day experiment.

Each player was assigned to conduct themselves during the duration of that afternoon practice session as one of their teammates. *So instead of playing how YOU normally play, James, you'll play how Scott plays. Mark, you will play as if you're Ben. Tucker, your job is to play the way you see Wayne play every day. Replicate the things he does well, and the things he messes up, so he can see his performance through your eyes.* The coach went down the line through all of his players, assigning each player to specifically be someone else for that practice. This, the coach explained, is how each one of you will see your mistakes demonstrated by your teammates instead of hearing it from me.

Tucker was a below-average player at best, who only occasionally played in the games. On this day for this experiment, however, Tucker had been assigned to act as a teammate who happened to be the best player on the team. That day, Tucker said, he played basketball better than he ever had, and better than he has been able to any day since. All because he had no choice but to "fake it" and make it as real as he possibly could.

Tucker did it because he was told to and was following his coach's instructions. You must choose to, and force the practice upon yourself.

The Super-You: What Your Success Will Be And Look Like

The following are your visions. Read and re-read these to internalize the feelings and thoughts that go with the vision. This chapter is your guide to Super-You-ness, and reminds you of who you are — now, and moving forward.

You Are The Person You Have Always Envisioned Yourself, Deep Down, To Be. You look in the mirror and you like what you see. You made your vision into reality. You think back to the days when this person in the mirror was just a dream, and feel the euphoria of knowing that you have become that exact person.

You Do All The Things You Always Dreamed Of Doing, The Way You Want To Do Them. There is no reason to hold back anymore. You made the conscious decision to be the best version of you, and the best version of you does not limit themselves. You do what you want to do and make no apologies for it. If this makes other people uncomfortable, that is their problem, not yours.

People Look Up To You, Come To You For Advice, And Aim To Emulate You. You are a role model for many people now, whether you choose to be one or not. There are people who you don't even know, for whom you are an example. This doesn't make you nervous at all, because you know you have earned that position in people's minds. You live every moment knowing that you are paving the way for many to follow behind you.

You Feel No Fear Or Timidity In Trying Something New. You have become successful *because of* the failures you've endured. They made you tougher, more resourceful, and smarter for the future. The fact that you are unafraid of failing is exactly what makes you successful: you perform with no fear of failure. Whatever does happen, you know you will find a way over or around it.

You Volunteer To Go First, Out In Front, Making It Easier For Everyone Else To Follow. You are the example-setter. You step up and go first, setting the stage for everyone else to follow behind you. Any issues that confront the group, the group knows they have a safety net: that you'll find a way to overcome it. Knowing this takes all of the pressure off of everyone else, allowing your followers to perform at their best. You carry all the pressure on your own shoulders, because you can handle it.

When You Encounter Success, You Don't Downplay It, Slow Down Or Coast. You keep going because that success makes you want even more. As soon as you reach an accomplishment, you're already thinking about your next one. The last one is history and you don't live in the past. You don't live in the future either — what you're doing right now is the only place you can achieve success. Which means you can't afford to slow down or take a rest. There is always something out there that you can achieve, and if it's not in front of you, you're looking for it.

When There Is A Challenge Facing You Or Your Group, You Don't Dwell On The Problems Or Sit Around Offering Suggestions. You never waste time or energy. You decide on a plan of action and take that action, without asking questions. A person who knows where he is going will compel others to follow, without having to say a word.

Practices For Building Your Confidence And Putting It To Work For You

The following steps are your easy-access handbook to confidence. Follow them and the self-assurance that results will compel people to follow you.

Visualize the Future You. Think deeply about who and what you'll be five, ten, fifteen years from now. Envision the way you will walk, talk and listen. Think about the clothes you'll wear and the cars you'll drive. What do you eat and why? Who are your friends and what do they value about you? What do people say about you when you're not around? How does your family feel about you and your life? What's your reputation in your business or on your team or within your company and how did that reputation develop? The deeper and more clearly you can see your future, the closer you place yourself to actualizing it.

Change The Way You Walk. This is not a metaphor, and we have discussed this earlier. The way you carry your body literally affects how you feel about yourself. The way you carry yourself tells people a lot about you; many will make a first and final decision about you based on what your body communicates. Take long, intentional strides. Walk like you have somewhere to be, and like you know exactly where that is. Keep your arms to your sides and let them sway naturally with your stride. Keep your head up and your gaze forward. Push your shoulders back while maintaining a natural gait, and keep your chin up and chest forward. It is nearly impossible to feel timid or depressed or sad when you mimic and practice this display, the body language of confidence.

Move Boldly Forward. The Super You does not calculate the possible pitfalls of a bold action before taking it. Worrying about what might go wrong is the exact opposite of boldness. The Super You does not worry about the future, which is never certain. You focus on the moment and deal with problems *when and if* they happen, not focusing on the possibility before it happens. Bold behavior makes people get out of your way. It puts people on their heels, in awe and in trepidation of your next bold maneuver. The presence and energy of a bold individual draws people in like a magnet. How would you like to have that effect on people? You can do this by adopting a bold attitude, which starts in your thoughts, and manifests itself in your words and actions. Most people are timid, worrying about what other people think of them and what might happen if they go too far beyond their limits. Boldness does not recognize limits. Take the daring thoughts that you have always had and be bold: put a few into action, and see what happens. The energy that accompanies bold action is both intoxicating and awe-inspiring.

Speak Up. When you speak, your non-verbal cues such as tone, volume and voice inflection tell people much more about you than your actual words. Make sure your throat is clear, and drink some water before you talk. Make sure your words are heard, the first time.

Decisions Over Suggestions. When a group is faced with a challenge, the fairly confident people will offer suggestions. The Super You is more than fairly confident, and also does more than suggest. You make decisions, and take action on those decisions without asking permission. There's a term we give to people who make decisions and take action while others wait to see what everyone else will do: Leaders. The Super You is a Leader.

Directions Over Questions. When there is something you need done and you have people at your disposal, tell them what you want done and/or how you want things done. Don't poll the group to see what everyone else thinks. When you are in charge, TAKE charge and put yourself in power. Power is never *given* to people, it is *taken*. Contrary to what some will tell you or what you may think, most people would rather be told what to do than be left to their own devices to make decisions. The Super You takes charge.

Eye Contact Matters. Eye contact is a simple, unconscious gage of a person's confidence level. I don't know any highly confident people, and definitely not any who have tapped into their Super You, who have trouble making and maintaining eye contact in conversation. Look at people when you talk to them and when they're talking to you. One experiment I read about from Tim Ferriss is to make eye contact with everyone you come across for a day, holding eye contact until *they* break it. If, on the rare occasion someone gets defensive and appears to take offense, just say, "Sorry, I thought you were someone I know." You'll find that 99% of people will break eye contact before you. This is a confidence building tactic that really works.

Renewing Your Confidence When Needed

Despite all your best efforts, there will be times when your confidence lags. Something goes wrong in your life. You don't perform at the level you expected to or that you knew you could. Someone says or does something to you that shakes your positive vibes. You look at your current circumstances and feel low about what you see around you.

It happens, and it will not stay that way.

These practices are for those times. Keep this list handy. Even better, let these ideas soak into and become part of you.

Gather Physical Reminders Of Your Past Happiness, Confidence And Success. These things matter. Objects, pictures, trophies, a lucky shirt — all of these things mark moments in your mind. Seeing these objects reminds you about the moments that made you feel good and unbeatable and Super (You) confident.

Find Sounds, Such As Audio Recordings, And Music, That Get You Into Your Zone. You already know how music or listening to certain things can change your whole mood. At any time of the day you may hear something that triggers a certain feeling. You have music you like listening to when you're driving. Songs you play when you're in the shower. Playlists for when you go for a run or when you're in the gym. How about a Confidence Playlist? Title it what you want, and put together a list of songs that put you in supremely confident, Super-You state of mind. At times you may change songs in and out of the playlist. You may not need it every single day, but it would be damn sure nice to have for when you do, right?

Remind Yourself Of Who You Are And What You've Done. You've had many successes in life. Those objects you keep around from above remind you of that. And just like you did it before, you can do it again. You're not a person who lives in the past, only able to talk about past achievements in lieu of doing something now, but there's nothing wrong with reminding yourself -- or others -- about what you've done.

Revisit Your Winning Energy. Think about the idea that sparked one of your best accomplishments. Or the energy you had that led to that idea, or some action that was a big victory for you. What was your thought process at the time? What were you feeling? Thinking deeply about these things can produce that same energy, and spark more ideas.

Get Angry About Letting Your Confidence Slip Even For A Second. You know better than to allow this. You're a leader. People look to you for reassurance when *they* feel doubt about themselves. That doesn't mean that you never can experience those same feelings. You are a human, after all, but your position in this world affords you much less of that luxury than most. This is the position of the Super You. If it does happen, use anger, a very powerful emotional fuel, against the fact that you allowed yourself to slip for even a moment. How *dare* doubt and insecurity even *think* about intruding into your mind's garden! Take it personally and use that energy towards what you *do* want.

Conclusion

The Super You ~~is~~ was the version of you that you ~~are~~ were afraid of being.

Confidence can be summed up in one phrase: Belief in yourself. You know what you have done and what you can do. When there's something new that you haven't done before, you can afford to lend confidence to yourself.

The Super You is this confidence, taken as far as it can be taken. Your energy seeps into everyone around you, and they instinctively follow your lead. You command respect and attention, walk boldly into new situations, and set an example for others to follow.

The Super You is the best version of the most confident and successful You, who doesn't shy away from achieving even more.

The Super You is the You that you no longer hold yourself back from becoming and expressing. You understand that this attitude will draw attention and that some may not understand nor relate to you, and that pushes you even further. You know that by embracing the Super You, you are separating yourself from some people who are uncomfortable with finding the Super within themselves, and that's OK with you. The Super You doesn't dim its own star so others can shine brighter. You set the example and let them come to where you are. The Super You doesn't lower her standards, she sets the standards.

Shine On.

[Next Steps] Texting Community: Your Secret Weapon To Connect With Me Directly!

I've opened a texting community where you can talk with me directly --

● **Get your questions and challenges answered** so you can always have support -- which means help is just a text away

● **Receive special content and updates** so you're always in-the-know about what's happening and what's next which means you're part of the inner circle

● **Know about events I'll be doing and places I'll be** so you can join meet-ups and attend live events: be in the room when things are happening

All you have to do is text me at 1.305.384.6894 (or just visit http://DreAllDay.com/Text) and add me to your phone, then I'll add you to mine, and you're in!

[Next Steps] The Exact Steps To Learn The Work On Your Game Philosophy In Just 25 Minutes Per Day… Guaranteed + FREE!!!

I specialize in helping people develop, show off, and get paid for your GAME. PERIOD.

Work On Your Game:
1) **Discipline:** Show up day after day to do the work.
2) **Confidence:** Put yourself out there -- boldly and authentically.
3) **Mental Toughness:** Continue showing up and putting yourself out there, even when the success you've expected hasn't yet happened.
4) **Personal Initiative:** Be a go-getter and make things happen instead of waiting for things to happen.

If you need to remove mental blocks that stop you from utilizing your skills... if you are serious about realizing your full potential... and want to know you've made the most of your life, then this is the MasterClass for you. And it's DAILY and 100% FREE.

Listen (and find links to all your favorite platforms) at http://WorkOnYourGamePodcast.com

[Next Steps] Get The Book Bundles

With so many books, it can be hard to know which book to get or to read next. We made it easy for you though -- just grab my books by the bundle and save yourself a lot of time!

Since I'm always writing, go to http://WorkOnYourGame.com to see what's in each bundle and choose what's best for you.

1. **Bulletproof Bundle:** Your mindset foundation
2. **Mental Game Advanced Bundle:** The next level for your mental game
3. **Leadership Bundle:** Translating your Mental game into interactions with others as a leader people will want to follow
4. **Story & Sales Bundle:** Telling your story and getting buy-in from the people you live and work with
5. **Overseas Blueprint Bundle:** For the professional player who wants an opportunity to make a living from your talent
6. **Basketball Workbook Bundle:** For the basketball player who needs to master your game and skillset both mentally and physically

[Next Steps] Bulletproof Mindset 2.0

This is my deepest course and the most comprehensive mindset training you can get anywhere. Bulletproof Mindset 2.0 promises to equip you with consistent, unbreakable mental game tools that will help you handle all of life's inevitable challenges -- not only from the outside world, but also from within.

Some of what you'll get in **Bulletproof Mindset 2.0**:

Unbreakable Mental Toughness which helps you handle life's challenges in stride so nothing breaks your flow or slows you down ever again

"Super You" - Level Confidence and self-belief that you and everyone else can feel so people see and treat you the same way YOU see you: as your highest and best self

Locked-In Focus so you can give your attention to one thing at a time and see it through to completion so you're never frazzled or overwhelmed by circumstances like most people

Consistent Discipline so you're able to finish everything you start, being steady and reliable so you can be a finisher who gets things DONE consistently

Bulletproof Communication Skills so you can get your point across every time without equivocation so people respect you and your word as they know you mean what you say

Learn more about **Bulletproof Mindset 2.0** and get started at http://WorkOnMyGame.com/Bulletproof

About The Author: Dre Baldwin

In just 5 years, Dre Baldwin went from the end of his high school team's bench, to the first contract of a 9-year professional basketball career. While playing professional basketball, Dre pioneered new genres of personal branding and entrepreneurship via an ever-growing content publishing empire.

Dre started blogging in 2005 and began publishing videos to YouTube in 2006. He has published over 8,000 videos and amassed 136,000+ subscribers, his content being consumed over 73 million times to date.

Dre's daily Work On Your Game Podcast MasterClass has over 1,700 episodes and more than 3 million downloads.

Dre has given 4 TED Talks on Discipline, Confidence, Mental Toughness & Personal Initiative and has authored 28 books. He has appeared in international campaigns with Nike, Finish Line, Wendy's, Gatorade, Buick, Wilson Sports, STASH Investments and DIME Magazine, amongst others.

A Philadelphia native and Penn State alum, Dre lives in Miami, Florida.

More By Dre Baldwin

Buy A Game

The Mirror Of Motivation

The Super You

The Mental Handbook

The Overseas Basketball Blueprint

100 Mental Game Best Practices

101 Content Ideas

Dre Philosophy Vol. 0

The Insta-Philosopher

25 Conversation Starters

25 Reasons to Quit Worrying

55 Daily People Skills

Ask Yourself A Better Question

The Seller's Mindset

The Mental Workbook

Work On Your Game

The Daily Game

Basketball: The 4 Essential Mental Game Tools

Basketball: Which Position Should You Play?

Basketball: Playing As Well As You Practice

Basketball: The 9 Essential Game Skills

Basketball: 30 Days To Tryouts

Bulletproof Mindset 1.0

30 Days To Discipline

The TRUTH About Overseas Basketball Exposure Camps

Basketball Agents: DECODED

Overseas Basketball Secrets

Work On Your Game System Manual

The Super You

#WorkOnYourGame

Printed in Great Britain
by Amazon

24660290R00040